EXERCISING TYPOLOGY

TABLE OF CONTENTS

INSTEAD OF THE PREFACE

Hello,

I am Alevtina Sedochenko, a business trainer with more than fifteen years of experience in marketing communications, advertising and management.

I have a history, sociology (M.A.) and psychology background.
I am a certified MBTI® practitioner (Step I, Step II).
I lead the iDevelopment project training, which aims to support people by using typology knowledge for trainings in communication, problem solving, teambuilding, personal development, career development and many other areas.

I typically work with diverse clients – businesses, students and individuals – who want to discover new opportunities through a better understanding of their own potential. After 2014, I started reaching a new audience - internally displaced people who are forced to leave their homes in the warship area of Eastern Ukraine. They need to start a new life from scratch and find their inner force, potential, and energy to survive and revive.

"Types discoveries" is a remarkable endeavor, although not easy, especially for people with no prior experience. Thus, I developed an interactive approach combining adapted psychology and personally created exercises. This approach enables typology to come to life in sharper – sometimes-funny – ways. Therefore, making it easier for the audience to understand, whilst bringing in various viewpoints.

This work resulted in the publishing of my book – "Trainers work-note" – in 2015 (for the time being, it is only available in Russian). It is a training planner that is composed of more than 50 exercises (with appendixes, examples, texts, worktables) and tests, and more than 80 stories, quotes, training plan examples and structured training planner tables, covering 5 themes – communication, teambuilding, problem solving, motivation and self-confidence.

In this book, I am happy to present you with new, user-proven exercises for psychological, business and typology trainings, consultations and coaching sessions.

Three reasons for me to write this book:

• I want to share my ideas with other people – practitioners in training, coaching and consulting who use Jungian typology, and who are interested in fresh contributions.

• I hope that feedback on the book can give me useful insights for further ideas and work.

• I believe the book will allow me to raise a budget in order to run practical trainings for people subjected to forced migration. This will help them understand and apply their potential and strengths. It will enable them to be more adaptive, to support themselves, and to be successful in what they do.

Three reasons for you to buy the book:

o   You get new, practical tools to make your group trainings and personal consultations more dynamic, interactive, interesting and exciting for your clients.

o   The exercise scenarios vary and their origins comes from different techniques: art-therapy, NLP, projective methods, etc. Thus, they can be of broad use and provide insightful outcomes.

o   You can mix the ideas from the book with your own, making your trainings unique, tailor-made and result oriented, in order to provide your clients with the highest level of satisfaction.

What you will find in the book:

✓   Sixteen exercises, four for each MBTI® dichotomy, that can also be used to illustrate cognitive, thinking and implementation approaches in non-typology trainings.

✓   Detailed descriptions of all exercises, including recommendations on the audience and group size, list of materials, necessary preliminary preparation, exercise flow, texts and worktables.

✓   Examples and explanations of how the exercises worked in my own groups with ideas of alterations, which you can implement in your training and coaching sessions.

I truly believe that this book will help all of us reach our goals and make others happier and stronger!

Thank you and best regards!

Sincerely,
Alevtina Sedochenko
ISFP, "practical helper"

Exercise №1 – "Energetic Punch"

This exercise can help point out the key characteristics of Extraverted and Introverted type's preferences by the participants themselves rather than the trainer. By making their "energetic punch", people explain the what, why and how of their energy. Different "punch recipes" can also reflect distinctions between the types.

Application:

- Adults and teenagers
- Group trainings and individual consultations

Materials and preparations:

- A3-A2 paper, markers

Description:

Before you start the exercise, convey to the participants a short story about the "punch".

"Punch" means "five" in Hindi, and a tradition states that 5 ingredients should compose a drink full of energy and harmony. Punches are usually made on the basis of juice or tea. However, when brought to Europe and America from India, the drink acquired a lot of diverse versions and recipes ...

Once the story explained, advise the participants to make their own recipe of the "energetic punch" by picking 5 main "ingredients" that convey energy and a sense of balance and comfort.

"Punch" ingredients may differ:
- People
- Situations
- Places
- Feelings
- Attitudes to life, etc.

Split the participants by Extraverts and Introverts and give them up to fifteen minutes to compose the "recipes". The optimal group size is made up of a maximum of five people.

Once the work is done, each group presents their "recipe" and explains what kind of ingredients – people, situations, places, characteristic, etc. – they have chosen, and why those ingredients bring energy, comfort and balance to them.

Discuss the "recipes" with the groups and point out the "ingredients" that particularly reflect or connect to characteristics of the Extraverted or Introverted type.

Notes:

The *Extraverted "punch"* may have the following "ingredients": *optimism, love, humor, communication, luck, etc.*
All the "ingredients" are generally about fun, communication and external actions.

The *Introverted "punch"* may have "ingredients" such as: *no irritant of any kind around, comfort, understanding, a sense of meaning and reasonable actions.*
All the "ingredients" compose a more reserved, calm "punch", concentrated on inner reflections.

Important! While discussing, point out that all "punches" are good, and have their "drinkers".

Adaptation options:

→   In groups of more than seven people, you may ask each participant to compose a personal "recipe" in five minutes and then continue the task in the group (E or I), discussing the "ingredients" mentioned by the participants, and pointing out the ones agreed within the group.

🖉 notes

_____

_____

_____

_____

_____

Exercise №2 – "Kindred Spirits"

This is an intriguing game that allows participants to understand their own preferences by using examples and solutions proposed by other people. The game can also give insights on the differences of people's (Extraverts and Introverts) reactions to the same situations.

Application:

- Adults and teenagers
- Group trainings

Materials:

- One set of stickers* for each participant
* The set consists of 2 small blocks (20x50 mm) of orange and blue stickers, the number of stickers in each block shouldn't be lower than the number of situations/questions you are going to use during the exercise.

Preparations:

- Prepare 5 to 10 situations or questions

Description:

Before you start:
- Make sure you know the participants' preferences (Extraversion/Introversion) since *for each round* of answers, you will have to pick a pair of participants (1 Extravert and 1 Introvert). However, the audience should not know the preferences of these people.
- Each participant should have an A4 sheet of paper and a set of blue and orange sticker blocks.

To start the exercise you should have at least five situations or questions ready to use for the rounds. Then, for each round, you should select a pair of participants – one Extravert and one Introvert.
Voice one of the situations, and ask the pair of selected people to comment on or elaborate on the situation.
When they are done commenting, ask each person from the audience to decide which of the two positions they connect the most with.
People who support the Extravert's point of view should put an orange sticker on their A4 sheet; those who support the Introvert's point of view should put a blue sticker on the sheet.

Do not tell people the meaning behind the color-coding, to ensure that they stay unbiased towards the positions voiced by the following pairs.

Continue with all the rounds you have planned.

In the end, all the participants should have a certain color composition on their paper, reflecting their point of view. People with a majority of orange stickers will most probably have an Extraverted preference whilst people with a majority of blue stickers will most probably have an Introverted preference.

Once all the situations have been presented, and the color-coding legend is revealed, ask participants from the different groups to share their comments on the situations and questions. Consequently, you will have a collection of different people's reactions to various situations. This offers a good illustration of the preferences, and gives people a better understanding of the existing diversity.

Notes:

1) "My colleague is aware of everything that is happening around, knows all the latest news and is always ready to share information with other people. I ..."
[Here the Extravert and Introvert representatives have to give their reaction to the situation or continue the sentence]

An *Extravert* may say the following:
- *"I enjoy speaking with this colleague to get stay informed"*
or
- *"I always find it interesting to communicate with this colleague"*

An *Introvert* may answer:
- *"I try to avoid meeting with this colleague, because he/she is so talkative"*
or
- *"I easily get tired when communicating with this kind of people"*

2) "My colleague is usually very shy during meetings and common discussions. I think ..."

An *Extravert* may say:
- *"He/she is not interested in the topic or does not have any opinion on It"*
An *Introvert* may answer:
- *"He/she is thinking about the topic or about his answer"*

Adaptation options:

→ For the "situations", you may also use quotes and ask people whether they support/don't support the approach, and explain why.
E.g.
An Extraverted approach, Richard Branson: *"Screw it. Let's do it"*.
An Introverted approach, Fran Lebowitz: *"Think before you speak. Read before you think"*.

Exercise №3 – "Building a House"

The exercise uses cards to help participants understand the preferences (Extraverts and Introverts).

Application:

- Adults and teenagers
- Group trainings and individual consultations

Materials:

- One set of cardsfor each group.
The set of cards should consist of 36 cards – 12 cards for each suit: location, house and neighbors
- A3-A1 paper, markers, cellar-tape

Preparations:

Prepare the set of cards – you can write words or use pictograms (try to avoid using pictures or photos as it may influence the choices).
* 2 cards are "jokers" – the participants may add their own options or examples from a movie, book, etc.

Cards examples:
Suit 1 - location
- The very center of a megapolis
- A touristic seashore town
- The center of the city near the main park
- A city shopping mall and cultural area
- Disneyland
- A quiet city downtown
- A village
- Mountains
- A sailing boat
- A desert island
- Your option* _____
- Your option* _____

Suit 2 - house
- A big hall, big kitchen, big backyard
- A pool with a party area
- A lot of place for guests
- A lot of windows and open spaces

- A glass ceiling
- No open spaces, each person has their own space in the house
- A garden with a lot of trees and plants
- A library with a home cinema
- A small patio or barbeque area with a nice view
- A loft with a telescope
- Your option* _____
- Your option* _____

Suit 3 - neighbors
- Active people with a lot of interests and hobbies
- People who like to go to parties and entertainment
- People who have the same interest as us, such as _____
- Open, hospitable people
- People with extravagant and unusual hobbies and interests
- People who travel a lot, they are usually absent but are interesting to talk to when available
- Quiet people with a tempered lifestyle
- People whom we can get in contact with, if needed
- No "next door" neighbors but there are neighbors living in the area
- No neighbors at all
- Your option* _____
- Your option* _____

Description:

Split the participants by Extravert and Introvert preference. The ideal group size has up to five people. *Note* - you may have several groups with the same preference, which is good, as it gives you more examples to illustrate their characteristics.

Ask the groups to "build a house" in 15 minutes.
In order to do that, each group receives one set of the cards. They may use the cards – only five cards from each suit – and may also add their own visions of "the most comfortable house".

After the work is done, each group presents their "house", based on the cards and additional ideas of the participants, and explains why they consider their "house" as "the most comfortable" one.

Ask people to explain their choices, and run a short group discussion on similarities and differences between each preference.

Adaptation options:

→   You may change the cards' content or add your own options.
Please note that the options in one suit should be equally split between both preferences; if you add the option to make more cards in one suit, you should also add an option in the other suits.

`Exercise №4 – "Art Gallery"

This exercise is very good to start the group training – its helps getting people acquainted and connected in a comfortable, relaxed atmosphere. It also helps the participants understand their preferences by expressing themselves through metaphors and associations.

Application:

- Adults and teenagers
- Group training

Materials:

- Up to 4 pairs of collages on A1-A2 paper, 6-8 sticker blocks (20x50 mm) of different colors, and A4 paper

Preparations:

Prepare at least 3 pair of collages (1 pair = 1 "Extravert" collage and 1 "Introvert" collage)

The collages can be organized and designed in different ways:

"Lifestyle" collages: working environment, leisure time, ideal place for life/relaxing, etc.
You may put pictures, photos, ideas that reflect the Extraverts' and Introverts' visions.

"Attitudes" collages: quotes, jokes, short thoughts or dialogs, "tags clouds", etc.
E.g.:
Extraverted quote - "Screw it! Let's do it!" (Richard Branson)
Introverted quote – "I'm in no hurry: the sun and the moon aren't, either" (Alberto Caeiro)

Extraverted short thought – "It turns out, there are a lot of people whom I do not know at this party. Excellent, I will go talk with people, make new friends, connections, and get some interesting information!"
Introverted short though – "It turns out, there are a lot of people whom I do not know at this party. Well, let me go and find somebody with whom I can have an easy-tempered talk about things that are interesting for both of us".

"Mixed" collages – use elements of the "lifestyle" and "attitudes" collages

Without particular directive, put the collage pairs on the walls of the room, or another place where people can move freely. Ensure there are an equal number of Extraverted and Introverted collages. On each collage, put small removable stickers of a certain color. Also, put the corresponding color mark (on one of the top corners) in order to correlate removable stickers to its collages. The number of stickers on each collage should not be less than the number of participants.

Description:

When the preparation is finished, ask the participants to walk around the collages and take one of the removable stickers from a collage they like. Afterwards, people should put their stickers on an individual A4 paper. They can add their thoughts and reflections on the same A4 paper.

When the group has finished with the sticker collecting, reveal the color-coding legend - which colors belong to Extraverted and which ones belong to Introverted collages.

It may happen that people have both Extraverted and Introverted stickers. It is a good demonstration that we all have both Extraverted and Introverted preferences, but one of them is more clearly defined than the other.

Please, note
! You should stay neutral in your attitudes while composing the collages – do not show your personal preference in the collage.
! All collages should be positive and have the same picture or word etc.

🖉 notes

_____

_____

_____

_____

_____

_____

Exercise №5 – "Understanding Basho"

Matsuo Basho is a Japanese poet of the Edo period (17th century). He is famously known as a great master in unfolding the world and feelings through a few simple elements in his haiku.

His poetry leaves people a lot of space for imagination and individual understanding of the scene.

Therefore, we will take Basho's haiku as a way to exercise Sensing and Intuition, and show participants how the same pictures, words and symbols may be de-coded differently by people of different preferences.

Application:

- Adults and teenagers
- Group training and individual consultation

Materials:

- Flipcharts or whiteboard, markers (for group training)

Preparations:

- Print out 1 copy of the Basho haiku for each group

Haiku examples:

For a lovely bowl
let us arrange these
flowers ...
Since there is no rice
***

Glorious the moon ...
therefore out thanks
dark clouds
Come to rest our necks
***

Silent the old town . . .
the scent of flowers
floating . . .
And evening bell
***

Description:

Split the participants by preference (Sensing and Intuition), in groups of 3-5 people. Give the same haiku to each group and ask them to present their vision and understanding of the poetry.

Usually, it takes up to 10-15 minutes for the groups to finish the task.

When all the groups are ready, let them present their approach of "understanding Basho" to the other participants.

Notes:

It is very interesting to see the specific approaches and general differences of Sensing and Intuitive participants when perceiving and interpreting the same information.

Thus, in the "lovely bowl" haiku, the *Sensing* approach *would most probably be based on playing with facts – bowls, flowers, rice - and practical approaches. People might put the flowers in the bowl. As there is no rice to put in it, why not make a vase from the bowl?*

The *Intuits* might employ another approach such as *trying to develop the idea or scenario further, using associations and symbols – the bowl may symbolize there is a pair of lovers, and they had a lovely evening ...*

Usually, the *Sensing* participants are *quite fast in finishing the task and have a common vision*, whilst the *Intuits* have *more debates on the options and might not come to a consensus regarding the common vision.*

It would be useful to point out the characteristics of participants' preferences based on their approaches to perceiving the information. It will help them better understand the differences.

notes

Exercise №6 – "Party Time"

Funny exercise that aims to activate interactions between participants and boost potential for idea generation. It helps them understand the mode of contribution that each preference can bring to a common discussion or brainstorm.

Application:

- Adults and teenagers
- Group trainings

Materials:

- Flipchart or whiteboard, markers
- A video recording opportunity would be a plus, and can make the exercise more dynamic

Preparations:

No special preparation is needed; you just have to ensure that enough space is available for groups to work independently, or at least for them not to interfere with each other too much.

Description:

Split the participants by preference (Sensing and Intuition) in groups of 5-7 people. Each group needs an observer who follows the discussion and makes notes regarding its flow. The observer is optional if you record the exercise.

The groups are given the task to develop a party idea, starting from the phrase:
"Let's do the party on a sky-scraper's roof!"
The participants speak one after the other, and each member of the group may only say one sentence per turn.

The game is quite intriguing as the participants not only need to produce their own ideas in a conveyer mode, they also need to develop a common vision, based on each others' input, with no opportunity to discuss it.

After 5 to 7 minutes, the game is over, and the groups have to present their party ideas together with the observer. The observer helps them retrace the discussion flow, and shares his observations.
In case of recording, you may use the video to point out distinctive characteristics of each preference.

Notes:

Usually, *Sensing* parties are *less innovative, but full of detail, very practical and easy to manage.*
The *Intuits* tend to *have "crazier' and crisper ideas, but not all of them are easy to implement.*

Adaptation options:

→ You may propose any other "starting point" as an idea generator, to respond to the audience or training goals.
→ You may also use the exercise as a brainstorm technique to develop real tasks or working situations in case the participants are colleagues.

🖊 notes

_____

_____

_____

_____

_____

_____

_____

_____

Exercise №7 – "Describing a Story"

This exercise helps participants understand how people with different preferences characterize the same information.

Application:

- Adults and teenagers
- Group trainings

Materials:

- Flipchart or whiteboard, markers

Preparations:

Print out (for each group) control points of a story. This will enable groups to follow the main thread of the story without repeating it. (You can also place them on a flipchart)

Example of a Story:

Old man Mazay once told us a story about his "rabbit adventure". There were high water levels in the countryside. He went for some firewood on a small boat. There was water everywhere on the way but suddenly he saw a small plot of land full of rabbits. Mazay took the rabbits on board of his boat and followed his route. Then, he saw a log with a dozen of rabbits. Mazay hooked on the log and trailed it along.
The whole village laughed at him upon his return. When Mazay moored his boat, the rabbits ran in different directions at top speed; only two couples were left, and they were totally wet and very weak. Mazay put them in a sack and took them home. Finally, they got dry and warm and Mazay let them out the next morning.
(Based on one of the poems on Nikolay Nekrasov)

Control points
Old man Mazay, high water, rabbits, log, village laughed, rabbits run, rabbits left, wet and weak, sack, took them home, let the rabbits out.

*Do not choose a very famous story and do not read a story twice so the participants can employ their imagination and produce their own interpretation of the story.

Description:

Split the participants by preference (Sensing and Intuition) in groups of 3-5 people.
Read a short story and give the groups the control points.

Ask the groups to present their own vision of the story in 10-15 minutes. No other guidelines should be given, to ensure the participants are free in their expression.
After the task is completed, ask the groups to present their stories about "old man Mazay and the rabbits".

Notes:

It can be very interesting to see how different types of preferences interpret and present the story.

Usually, *Sensing* participants are very *exact in the details (e.g. number of rabbits), and follow the scenario based on the control points. Their own additions are also about details and items.*
The *Intuits avoid details; they may neglect the control points and tend to change the scenario. They might also add new characters or plotlines.*

There was an Intuits group in my practice that even presented the story as a theatrical play ☺

✎ notes

_____

_____

_____

_____

_____

_____

Exercise №8 – "Describing Objects"

This exercise helps participants understand how people with different preferences perceive the same objects, and how those different objects are characterized by people of Sensing and Intuition preferences.

Application:

- Adults and teenagers
- Group trainings

Materials:

- Set of objects* (e.g. apple, orange, chocolate bar, list of A4 paper, napkin and color band appr. 50 sm long) + boxes of different colors or shapes.
*The number of object sets and boxes should be the same as the number of groups, 1set of objects in a box per a group.

Preparations:

Put a set of objects in each box. The participants should not see what is inside before they start the exercise.
The exercise requires a private space for each group. Groups should not see each other during this exercise.

Description:

Split the participants by preferences (Sensing and Intuition) in groups of 3-5 people.
Give each group a box with, inside of it, the set of objects.
The participants should not open the boxes until they go to their private areas to complete the task.

The task for each group is to analyze the set, and propose their own vision of what it represents.
The groups are free to express their understanding, and can do as they wish with the objects.

Groups go to the separate rooms and work for 15-20 minutes.
It is worth to visit the rooms and watch the process - you can catch good examples of and insights on the work of different groups.
When the groups are done with the task, they should put the objects back in their boxes and close them before entering the common training space where they will present their "pictures".

Notes:

Different groups usually present their sets in different ways.

Thus, *Sensing* participants try to:
- Describe *details of the set (shape, color).*
- Give some *rational and useful application of the set* (vitamins, energy, part of a lunch box, etc.).

Intuits try to:
- Employ *patterns or symbols when analyzing ("an apple is a symbol of ...").*
- Organize the *objects in a still-life pattern or use them creatively (e.g. they cut the fruits or break the chocolate bar).*

People might be very impressed to see that the same objects generate different interpretations and ideas.

Adaptation options:

→ You may compose your own set.

→ You may ask the participants not to mention the objects during the presentations, and once all groups are done with the presentations, ask them to show their sets. It might be more intriguing, but more difficult for the participants to make their presentations.

notes

_____

_____

_____

_____

_____

Exercise №9 – "Two Solutions of One Problem"

This is one of the best exercises to use for corporate trainings or with a team of colleagues. The exercise is based on a number of working situations that need to be resolved by people of Thinking and Feeling type. So, the participants may not only understand the difference between the preferences, but also see how they are executed in real situations.

Application:

▪ Adults
▪ Group trainings

Materials:

No special materials are needed

Preparations:

Print 1 copy of the same situation for each group. To make the exercise more dynamic, you need to prepare 2-3 situations.

Examples of situations:

1) It is the first day at work of an employee. He made a commodity display on his own in the sales room, but it turned out to be different from what you expected. You relied on his experience and expertise, and therefore, had not provided him with detailed Instructions. You need to talk to the person about this issue. How would you approach the situation?

2) Your colleague is the boss' favorite. He usually interrupts other people during the meetings, and tries to impose his own point of view. This behavior does not allow others to express their vision.
You need to talk to this colleague about the issue. How would you approach him to solve the situation?

3) Your boss likes to push his point of view on almost every issue. Sometimes, his decisions do not resolve the problem, although responsibility for his proposed solution may be imposed to other people. You are in charge of quite an important project, and your boss tries to micro-manage it.
You need to communicate this issue to your boss. What would be your approach?

Description:

Split the participants by preference (Thinking and Feeling), in groups of 3-5 people.

Give each group a copy of the same situations. The groups have the task to propose solutions to the situations. It usually takes up to 15-20 minutes to cope with 2-3 situations.

When the groups are done with the task, they present their solutions to all participants.

Notes:

Usually, *Feeling* participants try to:
- Use a more *friendly approach: they speak with their colleagues in an informal setting (* "cup of coffee'), build a *closer contact before discussing the issue* (#1 & #2) and "find an appropriate moment" (#3).
Thinking participants try to:
- Use a more *formal communication method, create procedures and rules* (# 1 & #2) and put forward *convincing arguments* (#3).

It might be beneficial for the group of colleagues to discuss other examples from their own experience, in order to bring their knowledge to life.

Adaptation options:

→   You may compose your own situations in line with the group specifics – sales, marketing, business development, etc. It will give the training more vivacity and can bring a sense of "tailor made" arrangement.

notes

Exercise №10 – "Fiery Speeches"

This exercise allows for the understanding of motivational approaches of people with Thinking and Feeling preferences. The exercise is of particular help in trainings on leadership, communication or teambuilding.

Application:

- Adults and teenagers
- Group trainings

Materials:

No special materials are needed

Preparations:

Print 1 copy of the same situation for each group – in case you have 2 groups (1 Thinking and 1 Feeling) you will need 2 copies, and in case you have more groups, then you will need more copies.
It is recommended to give the participants only one situation for this exercise, so they can concentrate on analyzing the topic and generating arguments.

Examples of situations:

1) Your company (or department) is facing a tough period – you lost some big clients and your sales volume are down. Some of your key managers are looking for other jobs outside of the company. You are confident that if they stay with the company, you may overcome the difficulties and attract more clients soon. If they go, you can still survive the situation, but it will take more time, effort and investment.
You need to convince the managers to stay.
What would your approach be?
How are you going to influence their decision?

2) Your company (or department) has a lot of new employees. People are active and willing to interact, but some processes are uncoordinated, and thus, not effective.
You want to make the teamwork less chaotic and more fruitful.
What would your approach be for activating the teambuilding potential?
How would you motivate people to work more effectively?

3) Your team lost a competition. The team did its best, but a competitor won the prize. Your team members are discouraged and demotivated.
You need to talk to them and reassure them to achieve further work and victories.
(This situation works well with teenagers)

Description:

Split the participants by preference (Thinking and Feeling), in groups of 3-5 people.
Give each group a copy of the same situation.
The groups are asked to analyze the situation and to prepare a short motivational speech. It is important for the groups to define 3 to 5 arguments – this will help participants understand the differences in the motivational approach in disregard to the general speech delivery mode.

Inform the participants that they do not need to polish their speech too much. The priority is for the audience to understand their approach and arguments.

The groups may need 15-20 minutes to complete the task.

When the groups have finished the task, they present their speeches and the arguments they consider to be most effective.

Notes:

Usually, *Feeling* participants try to *employ emotional arguments linked to the team, common work, and mutual aid*; for example, mentioning hard work but a good future, etc. They set up their *leading function as a part of the team, working together with others*. Their speeches are more *emotional*.

Thinking participants try to *use logic, "cause and effect" approach, and set up next steps*, *which would lead to success*. They tend to present themselves mainly as *sole leaders, bosses who give visions or instructions on how the team should perform*. Their speeches are *not as emotional* as of the Feeling groups.

It might be beneficial for the group of colleagues to discuss other examples from their own experience in order to bring their knowledge to life.

Adaptation options:

→   You may compose your own situations regarding the groups' specifics or addressing the issues relevant to the participants.
→   You may also give more time to prepare the speech, in order to make its delivery a real performance.
This will make the exercise more stimulating and dynamic. It can bring a sense of "tailor made" arrangement.
This approach works well for trainings on leadership, communication and motivation.

Exercise №11 – "Convince Me!"

This exercise permits the demonstration of arguments used by people of different preference in order to convince the audience or to achieve a goal.
A participant may grasp 2 sides of the situation – how he approaches the opponent and how the opponent might approach him.

Application:

▪ Adults and teenagers
▪ Group trainings

Materials:

No special materials are needed, but it is recommended to have some "gifts" - small and tasty things, such as chocolate bars or fruits in order to use them both for the exercise and as a snack afterwards.

Description:

Split the participants by preference (Thinking and Feeling), in groups of 3-5 people.
Tell the groups that you have a gift for them; in order to get it, they have to convince you to give the gift to them.
Actually, this is the task itself, and the groups may use any arguments and tactics of persuasion.

The groups should take 10-15 minutes to complete the task.

When the groups are done with the task, they present their arguments and mode of persuasion.

Notes:

Usually, *Feeling* groups primarily try to use:
- *"tête-a-tête"* approach;
- Arguments such as: *"we are good", "we are friends", "we always help you and will be helping", "we want this for another person who needs it", "we will do something good for you", "we'll share the chocolate with other people"*, etc.

Thinking participants primarily try to use:
- Arguments such as: *"we worked hard, had this and that result, so we deserve a reward", "we need something to boost our energy, to work better", "we give you something in return"*;
- They do not necessarily specify the approach, and can *take any opportunity that leads to the goal.*

Adaptation options:

→   You may use any kind of items as "gifts", but if you have something eatable, it may be a good addition to a coffee break ☺

→   You may also prepare your own situation as task, e.g. it may reflect some working situations or can be related to the audience issues, problems, needs, etc.

✏ notes

Exercise №12 – "Associations Fields"

This exercise uses an associative approach to show how the same terminology may have different meanings and different demonstrations for people of different preferences. It also helps the participants understand behavioral cues.

Application:

▪ Adults and teenagers
▪ Group trainings, individual consultations

Materials and Preparations:

No special materials and preparations are needed

Description:

Split the participants by Thinking and Feeling preference (groups of up to 3-5 people).
Ask the groups to formulate fields of associations on given topics, e.g.:
- Effective team
- Fair decisions
- Good boss

Usually, 2 topics can be done in 10-15 minutes.
Once the task is finished, the groups present their association fields.
Discuss the "association fields" with the groups and point out the associations that most link to the preferences.

Notes:

If you have taken the topic "effective team", you find that *Feeling* groups tend to stress on *teamwork, mutual aid, common understanding*, etc.

Thinking participants first of all point out *professionalism, a team of good experts, effective allocation of responsibilities*, etc.

Please, note that the "fields" of both groups may contain the same notions. However, it is important to look at the *prioritization and "weight" of the notions*.

Adaptation options:

→   For teenage groups, instead of "fields" you can use "tags" and ask people to point out their associations in the form of tag clouds.

Exercise №13 - "I'm an Alien in ..."

Light and funny exercise that activates group idea generation and helps understand Judging and Perceiving preferences.

Application:

- Adults and teenagers
- Group trainings, individual consultations

Materials and Preparations:

No special materials and preparations are needed

Description:

Split the participants by Judging and Perceiving preference (groups of up to 3-5 people).

Ask the groups to describe their day in a strange city, where they happened to have an unplanned stop.

It may take about 10-15 minutes for the groups to complete the task.

When the groups are done with the task, they present their stories.

Notes:

Judging groups are more disposed to:
- *Take unplanned conditions negatively*
- Try to find out how to *return back to the planned situation*
- Be *less open to discover new opportunities*
- Try to *arrange a new plan* or contact a travel office where they can find information or guidance

Perceiving participants are more inclined to:
- Easily *accept the change in plans*
- Discover *new opportunities in the occurring situation*
- *Take on an adventure* whenever they have the chance
- Walk *around the city with a map, but without guidance*

It may be interesting to have a discussion with the participants about the feelings they have when they find themselves in an unpredictable situation. On the other hand, *people can also share real stories of such a situation.*

Exercise №14 – "Attitudes Cards"

Good exercise to gain an understanding of the emotional state of people with Judging and Perceiving preferences, in different situations.

Application:

- Adults and teenagers
- Group trainings, individual consultations

Materials:

- "Attitude" cards set – 1 for each group

Preparations:

You should prepare the "attitude" cards. They can easily be made by printing words on a thick piece of paper. You can make a standard card size (6.3x8.8 mm) or make them any size you want.

Example of meanings for the "attitude" cards:

Positive		Negative	
Trust	Sympathy	Unacceptance	Incomprehension
Desire	Support	Irritation	Rejection
Pleasure	Optimism	Anxiety	Apathy
Determination	Readiness	Dissatisfaction	Uncertainty
Satisfaction	Cooperation	Reluctance	Resistance
Appreciation	Interest	Anger	Boredom
Order	Comfort	Regret	Nervousness
Confidence	Understanding	Tiredness	Uninvolvement
Joker*	Joker*	Joker*	Joker*

* The Joker is an empty card that allows the participants to put their own psychological states and emotions in case they could not find the right attitude written in the cards.

It is also helpful to use color-coding for the positive and negative cards in order to ensure that the participants and yourself, can easily sort them out when required.

You also need to print out 2 situations per group - the same ones for all groups.

Examples of situations:

1) You are a project manager.
Your client requires you to plan all the project details and to present a very detailed explanation in a specific format. He calls you on a daily basis and likes to have regular status-meetings even if the project is going smoothly and nothing unplanned has happened.

He does not like to change plans and to consider any other options, since the plan has been approved and the work has started.
You think that the plan may need to be adjusted and give him the proposal. The client scheduled a meeting about that for tomorrow ...

2) You are a project manager.
Your client considers a project as a "live" process that needs constant adjustments in order to be up to date. He calls every day to discuss new opportunities and potential improvements. He easily proposes and makes changes.
Today, the client called about a new project idea, he thinks the plan needs to be adjusted. He scheduled a meeting about that for tomorrow ...

Description:

Split the participants by preference (Judging and Perceiving) in groups of 3-5 people.
Give a set of "attitude" cards and 2 situations to each group. Ask the groups to give their attitude towards the situations using the cards. The participants have to pick up the cards that express their attitudes and emotions. They may take as many cards as they want from the set. If the set does not contain a state of mind they want to show, the participants can use an empty "joker" card to write the needed state.

It may take about 15-20 minutes for the groups to complete the task.

When the groups are finished with the task, they present their attitudes for each of the 2 situations.

Notes:

Judging groups usually view situation #1 as normal; they understand the client and use more positive cards when expressing their attitude. The *Perceiving* types use more negative cards for this situation.

With situation #2, the opposite is observed – the *Judging* groups are more negative, and the *Perceiving* groups are more positive – in the attitudes they express.

Adaptation options:

→   You may adapt the "state of mind" set by changing or adding meanings.
→   You may also add more "jokers" to give people more freedom to express themselves.

Exercise №15 - "Talks in Pencil"

This exercise is based on an art-therapy approach, and requires creative interaction between people with different preferences. It is less about differences, though, and more about understanding and finding ways to co-operate.
The exercise can be a very good closing activity in trainings.

Application:

- Adults and teenagers
- Group trainings

Materials:

- A2 or A1 paper, color markers

Preparations:

No prior preparation is needed

Description:

Split the participants in pairs (Judging and Perceiving). If you have an uneven amount of participants, compose a micro-team of 3 people in which 1 person should be of a different preference.

Give each person in the pairs or micro-group a marker of a certain color. No two markers of the same color should be given to the same pair/group and no changes are allowed in the markers' color.

People in the pairs or micro-groups are given the task to make a drawing. There is no specification given regarding what to draw.

However, the participants should work with the following *requirements*:

1) The drawing starts by a person with a *Judging* preference, and then switches to another member. People should keep drawing in succession;
2) One person cannot draw more than 3 lines of any type in one turn;
3) No verbal or non-verbal communication is allowed, people should try to understand each other through the process of drawing;
4) People make all drawings in fair copy; no rough drafts or drawing deletion is allowed. People can only transform the previous drawings by adding lines or simple elements.

It may take up to 15-20 minutes for the pairs or micro-groups to finish the drawing. You may also allow people to use more time, to finish the picture completely.

Then, people present their pictures and explain how they were made. It might be interesting to analyze the participants' input by tracing the colors used by each person.

Notes:

There are no distinctive outputs to be found in the results. However, you may notice that people with *Judging* preference predominantly *use straight lines and tend to model a structure*, while people with *Perceiving* preference mainly *use fanciful lines and put more elements as additions*.

An added value to the exercise may be to include a reflection:
- What did the participants feel and think during the exercise?
- What was irritating and what was comfortable, difficult and easy?
- When did they understand the idea of their common picture?

notes

Exercise №16 - "Two Tasks"

An interesting, combined approach that allows the participants to practice their Judging and Perceiving characteristics in one exercise.
The exercise has a creative element and is very good as a closing scene in the training.

Application:

- Adults and teenagers
- Group trainings

Materials:

Set #1 (for each team) - A3 and A4 paper, markers
Set #2 (for each team) - colored paper and carton, glue, scotch tape, scissors
Set #3 (for all teams) – toothpicks or small wooden skewers, small wooden or plastic bricks, small glass pebbles, or any other things you may consider interesting for the exercise (see description below).

Preparations:

Prepare the materials listed above in advance and in sufficient quantity for the teams to do the exercise (see description below).

Description:

Split the participants by preference (Judging and Perceiving) and create teams of 3-5 members. Give them the materials from Set #1.
Explain to them the following task: in 10 minutes, compose a plan for a big event (wedding, corporate Christmas party, company moving to a new office, etc.)

While people do the task, observe their method and take notes of their discussion (what ideas they propose, how they discuss and communicate, etc.). Do not pressure or help the participants.

After approximately 5-7 minutes, stop the task, even if the participants are not finished.

Give the groups Set #2 with a new task: build a house in 20 minutes. Do not specify the type of house, the place and any other details. The groups decide for themselves how it should be.

Approximately 5-7 minutes after they start working on the task, give the teams a portion of the materials from Set #3, e.g. - toothpicks. Do not mix the materials from Set #3, it should be one type of material given at once.

3-5 minutes later, give them another part of material from Set #3 (e.g. bricks). Give the subsequent part (the pebbles) after another 3 minute. Continue with this 3-minute interval until there are no more materials. The main reason for giving these items is to provide new "opportunities" during the process.

Once the distribution of all the materials from Set #3 is done, give the participants some extra time to finish the task. If need be, after 20 minutes, you can allow the participants to take some more time.

When the task is done, look at the groups' results from two perspectives – planning the event and creating the house. You might find some interesting outputs!

Notes:

Usually, the *Judging* teams are quite *accurate in the first part of the exercise – planning and structuring*. They have almost (or even entirely) finished their plans by the time you stop the task.
In the second task, they generally go *very fast, in a simple manner, almost not using any additional materials* (Set #3) that are given to them as unplanned opportunities. Keeping in mind that they were interrupted and did not totally complete task #1, the *Judgers try to finish task #2 as soon as possible to be in time.*

Teams with the *Perceiving* preferences are *not that accurate with task #1*. They spent *more time discussing opportunities*, and wrote fewer facts in their plans.

There was a group in my practice that only wrote one line – "to find an agency that can arrange everything" ☺ and spent all the rest of the time discussing on the type of party it could be.

In the second task, the *Perceivers* are *more creative and less time sensitive*. The participants usually *try several options for the house architecture and may try to create it in 3D*. The group *uses all the materials – opportunities – to make the house* and it's surroundings more elegant.

There was another group in my practice that used all the materials and then asked whether more would be given. When I told them that no other materials (opportunities) are available, the participants started to look for new materials (opportunities) independently. They used sugar cubes and flower-shaped biscuits from a coffee-break table to create a path to their house through the garden ☺

It is very *important in this exercise to stress on the specifics of every preference in a positive manner – point at the positive aspects of understanding their types* and give them insight on *how to use their strengths effectively*.

I WISH YOU BRILLIANT TRAININGS and HAPPY CLIENTS!

Best regards, your practical helper Alevtina Sedochenko